body beat

Ollie Tunmer

www.beatgoeson.co.uk

Front cover photographs courtesy of Oliver Winstone
Video footage courtesy of Jon Collins

ISBN: 978-1-5400-4425-9

Visit Hal Leonard Online at
www.halleonard.com

Contact us:
Hal Leonard
7777 West Bluemound Road
Milwaukee, WI 53213
Email: info@halleonard.com

In Europe, contact:
Hal Leonard Europe Limited
42 Wigmore Street
Marylebone, London, W1U 2RY
Email: info@halleonardeurope.com

In Australia, contact:
Hal Leonard Australia Pty. Ltd.
4 Lentara Court
Cheltenham, Victoria, 3192 Australia
Email: info@halleonard.com.au

Contents

About the Author

Ollie studied Drum Kit and Orchestral Percussion throughout his teens before focussing on Afro-Brazilian Percussion as part of his degree at Kingston University. During this time he also played with London School of Samba and the Rio de Janeiro carnival. On his return from Brazil, he joined Samba/Drum'n'bass ensemble Carnival Collective and performed at Glastonbury and numerous other club and festivals throughout the UK and Europe.

Ollie first worked with STOMP as a part of their workshop team, then as a cast member of their sister show *The Lost & Found Orchestra*, with whom he performed at a number of venues including the Sydney Opera House. He then joined STOMP as part of the London and European Tour casts.

Ollie then turned his focus to education and whilst completing his PGCE spent a short time teaching Percussion at the British School of Bahrain. He then taught Music in a secondary school, an experience which allowed him to develop skills transferrable to workshop facilitation.

He founded Beat Goes On in 2016 and has also appeared on BBC's *The Let's Go Club* and created a Body Percussion routine for a Rio 2016 Olympics pre-games trailer.

His latest live project is Sambaoke — 'mass karaoke with a live samba band!'. Visit **www.sambaoke.com** for details.

BEAT
GOES
ON...

Ollie is the director of 'Beat Goes On', a Percussion workshop company specialising in STOMP-style Body Percussion and Afro-Brazilian Percussion. They deliver workshops, teacher training and conference sessions, including at the Music & Drama Education EXPO, Music Mark conferences and for numerous music education hubs throughout the UK and abroad.

Beat Goes On's international work has included keynote presentations at the Latin American Heads Conference in São Paulo, BSME (British Schools in the Middle East)'s inaugural Music & Drama Conference in Dubai, Musical Futures Australia's 'Big Gig' in Melbourne, Little Kids Rock's 'Modern Band Summit' in Colorado, a residency at North London Collegiate School Jeju in South Korea and numerous events throughout Europe.

Alongside the STOMP-style Body Percussion and Afro-Brazilian Percussion workshops, Beat Goes On also work with Junk Percussion, Boomwhackers & Bamboo Tamboo and Body Percussion with literacy. The latter of these grew out of collaborations with literacy specialist Pie Corbett of Talk4Writing. These workshops involve exploring the rhythmic potential of spoken words and then adapting them to create Body Percussion routines. This fun, kinaesthetic approach builds pupil and teacher confidence with literacy and music alike, and is explained in this book.

For free downloadable resources, videos and all workshop, teacher training and conference enquiries please visit **www.beatgoeson.co.uk** and follow **@BeatGoesOnUK**.

Introduction

I love Body Percussion for many reasons. You can do it anywhere, any time, and it doesn't cost you anything. This accessibility and the energy it can produce makes it immediately gratifying but, like most things, it requires dedication to develop.

Body Beats is a selection of material I've incorporated over 20 (ish) years of delivering Body Percussion and other workshops. Whether you're an individual with a desire to develop your musical confidence and skills, or a teacher who would like to use more Body Percussion with your class, this is for you.

While the ideas are rhythm-based, we also use words in the form of what I call 'rhythmonics'. These are rhythms and mnemonics combined to create spoken phrases that act as memory aids and deepen the learning by incorporating key terms and vocabulary. There is also scope to sing these words, adding melodic and harmonic elements. For these reasons, the genre can be referred to not just as 'Body Percussion', but as 'Body Music'.

Alongside musical development, *Body Beats* also draws upon the kinaesthetic benefits of Body Music, providing opportunities for 'creative exercise', developing co-ordination and promoting well-being throughout schools and other communities.

This resource is most beneficial for children aged 6+ years and adults. If you work with younger children and people of all ages with special educational needs and disabilities, please contact us at **www.beatgoeson.co.uk** for suitable ideas and resources.

There are videos of everything that is covered so you can practise with me as much as you like before trying it with your friends/pupils/students! Feel free to adapt these ideas to suit your own learning/teaching contexts and let me know if you have any specific questions or suggestions for further developments — I'd love to hear from you!

Have fun, be creative and enjoy the journey!

Ollie Tunmer

Origins

Body Percussion/Body Music is the oldest form of human communication. It has been used in celebrations and gatherings for thousands of years and continues to develop around the world in a wide variety of musical contexts.

Its history has been, and continues to be, researched and documented by the ever-expanding global community it engages. You may wish to research these notable examples, including:

- Gumboot Dancing (South Africa)
- Armpit Music (Ethiopia)
- Saman Dance (Indonesia)
- Clog Dancing (UK)
- Step Dancing (Ireland)
- Flamenco (Spain)
- Hambone/Juba Dance, Stepping, Clogging (All USA)
- Tap Dancing (based on African, English, Scottish and Irish folk dances).

Famous examples of Body Percussion performance and education

Steve Reich's 'Clapping Music' (1972) develops the musical device of 'phasing'. The piece features one performer clapping an 'ostinato' repeated pattern (actually a West African bell line). The other performer claps the same pattern but periodically shifts or 'phases' by one beat. This continues until the phasing performer has realigned with the original pattern.

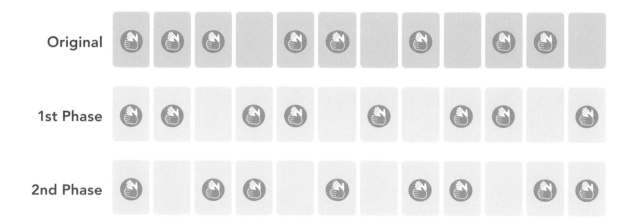

'Clapping Music' is one of the most famous examples of Body Percussion used in Western Classical music. Other more recent examples include Anna Meredith and David Ogle's 'Hands Free' (2012), which was premiered by the National Youth Orchestra of Great Britain, and 'Connect It' (2014) (also by Meredith and Ogle), commissioned for the BBC's award-winning *Ten Pieces* initiative performed by children throughout the UK. Beat Goes On designed a workshop based on elements from 'Connect It', the material of which is included on page 19.

The following groups have made significant contributions to the profile of Body Percussion internationally:

STOMP (UK) — originating from Brighton, this multi award-winning show has toured the world, won countless awards, appeared at the 1996 Oscars, the London 2012 Olympics closing ceremony, numerous TV adverts and has been incorporated into many music curricula.

Crosspulse (USA) — an art organisation founded by Artistic Director Keith Terry 'dedicated to the creation, performance and recording of rhythm-based, intercultural music and dance'. They also collaborate with local body music organisations to run the International Body Music Festivals.

Barbatuques (Brazil) — a performing group and developers of Body Music education, including contributions to the *Rio 2* film soundtrack and the Rio 2016 Olympics closing ceremony.

Beatboxing has also gained huge popularity thanks to artists including Rahzel, Shlomo, Reeps One, Kaila Mullady, Killa Kella and Beardyman.

Zoltan Kodály, Émile Jaques-Dalcroze and Carl Orff have all developed key methods which are implemented in music education internationally. All incorporate a strong focus of the development of body movement and rhythm. You can find more information by visiting **www.iks.hu**, **www.dalcroze.org.uk** and **www.orff.de/en/start-englisch**.

Sound symbols

POP   mouth pop

SHH   the 'shh' sound with your mouth

    click

clap

C clashy clap, with flat hands

B bassy clap, with cupped hands

A
X   crossed arm taps

SLD   hand slide

10   'high ten' your partner

SLP   slapping your neighbour's hand:
right hand is palm down and claps down, left hand is palm up and claps up

L-R   left hand moving across to high five the person on your right

R-L   right hand moving across to high five the person on your left

CH	chest	TH	accented thigh beat	L	left foot
L CH	left chest	R TH	accented right thigh	R	right foot
R CH	right chest	L TH	left thighs	SFL	shuffle forward on both feet
BLY	belly	R TH	right thighs	SLD	slide back on both feet
L BLY	left belly				stomp
R BLY	right belly				together
HIP	hips				

Exercises accompanied by video tutorials are marked with this symbol: ▶

To access this content, log into MyLibrary using the code provided on the inside cover.

Getting into the groove

Body Percussion combines many elements — pulse, rhythm, pitch, timbre, coordination, listening and the shifting of body weight. Some people are lucky enough to feel these elements instinctively, possibly through exposure to them since birth. Other people need to think about them a little more to progress.

Whichever you think you are, it might help to start by laying down a simple and solid rhythmic foundation from which you can develop. Here are a few exercises you can try:

Walking and breathing

- Walk on the spot, at a steady speed, and breathe in over a count of four steps, then out over the next count of four. Repeat this process, shut your eyes and be aware of how your walking and breathing relate to each other.
- Whilst doing this, add a clap or click to your second step and repeat a few times. Try this with your third and fourth step.
- Try the following sequence, repeating each stage four times, with a different sound for each number:

With your first step — clap
With your second step — chest
With your third step — thighs
With your fourth step — click/finger tap

Remember to keep breathing in for four steps and out for four steps.

Marking the pulse

Whenever you hear music, whether you've got the radio on in the kitchen or listening to your favourite playlist, try to mark the 'pulse'. Not all music has a clear pulse but lots of Rock, Pop, Dance and Jazz does, so these are good starting points.

- Most 'popular' music is 4/4 or 'common' time, which means we're counting four beats per bar/measure.

- Nod your head, tap your thighs, play 'air' drums — however you do it, try to keep in time with the pulse of the music.

- If you're listening to rock and pop music, which often has very clear beats on '2' and '4' (this is known as the 'backbeat', where the snare drum is often played), try to clap along.

- You'll only be playing two of the four beats, so try playing the '1' and '3' by tapping your foot. It's a bit of a test of coordination but starting with clapping all four beats then splitting them between hands and feet will make it easier.

Warm-up games and exercises

for individuals

With all of the following exercises, start slowly and gradually speed up, maintaining smooth flow as you go. Try varying the exercises by moving the beats played with your hands around to chest, belly, hips, etc. You could also move your feet outwards and inwards on the 'feet' beats.

01. Quavers/8th notes

02. Percussive triplets

02a. Percussive triplets

Try inverting these, so that the 'clap' moves away from the pulse.

12

03. Semiquavers/16th notes

04. Sextuplets

05. Speeding Up

Demonstration Video

06. On-beats and off-beats with feet

STOMP start their 'Hands & Feet' routine with each performer playing a different clapping rhythm, and a unison foot rhythm.

Start with this simple foot line:

Now try each of these hand lines on their own, one at a time:

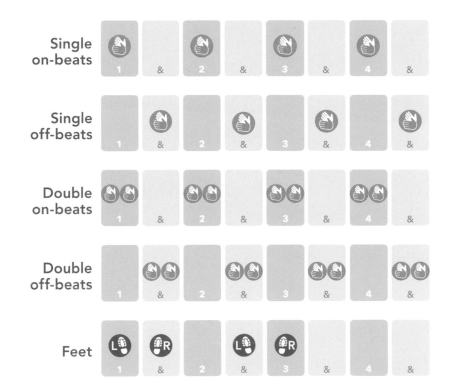

Then try combining the hand lines with the foot line — you may need to try it very slowly at first, identifying which clapped beats are played at the same time as a foot beat and which are separate.

07. In a group setting

Divide your group up and have each section playing a different hand line. You might need to mark the pulse by tapping your foot or nodding your head. Make a point of listening to each and getting different combinations of lines playing together — this will allow you to appreciate how the lines relate to each other.

Warm-up games and exercises
for groups

Here are some of my favourite rhythm games to develop confidence and coordination. They provide a foundation for composition and development of performance skills. Feel free to adapt them to support whomever you might be working with.

Call and Response

- Start with rhythms that fit over a count of four beats, as this will probably feel most familiar, and include variations of body sounds, rests and syncopation.
- Take turns to create the 'call' that everyone will play back. The response might be a direct repetition of the call, or you might decide you use a rhythmic response that is different to the call. Call and Response is used in many forms of folkloric music around the word.

On-beats and off-beats with feet: 1, 2, 3 pairs

This is a well-known game in drama education circles that can be used to develop ensemble skills.

Try the exercise in different stages:

- Start by saying each number, alternating with your partner as you go
- Replace the **1** with a **clap**, and continue saying **2** and **3**
- Replace the **3** with a **stomp**, and continue with the **clap** and saying **2**
- Replace the **clap** and **stomp** for different body sounds
- Try doing this as a group of many pairs. The leader could clap or play a cowbell to maintain a strong pulse. If someone makes a slight mistake, they can simply listen to the group and rejoin at the next **1** or **clap**.

This is how live performance works — mistakes do happen but it's how we deal with them that is important!

08. Ideas based on Ghanian circle clapping games

You could use this as a name game, with each person in the group taking it in turns to say their name on the **click** (beat four) and everyone else saying it back to them on the next **click**. Finger clicks can be substituted for tongue clicks or two finger taps.

You can add this to 'Marching' or 'Samba' feet:

Try playing either Version A or B four times then turning on the spot over a count of 8. Repeat the whole routine, accelerating gradually as you go — try to keep to groove going!

09. 1–8 Sound Sequence inspired by STOMP's 'Pipes' routine

In eight small groups, each group is given a number between 1–8 and chooses one percussive sound to play on their number, resulting in eight different sounds.

- Start with the groups whispering their number, starting with **1** through to **8** in a loop.
- Build the rhythm up with each group playing their sound on their number, until all are playing.
- Ask only groups with odd numbers, even numbers, prime numbers, etc. to continue to create new rhythmic patterns.
- Vary dynamics and tempi.
- Try replacing percussive sounds with sung notes of a scale to create a melodic ostinato (repeated pattern).
- Shutting your eyes can help to internalise the feel of the pulse.

1, 2, 4 rhythm game named because you learn
individually (1), in pairs (2), then quartets (4)

This is my take on a game taught to me by Beat Goes On facilitator Mika de Oliveira. It's a lovely combination of body sounds and development of coordination. It requires real team work to achieve a great sounding groove!

Try jumping instead of stomping at the beginning of line 2. Be careful — the sound occurs when you land, so you'll need to anticipate the jump.

10. 1: Individual

Learn the two line pattern.

11. 2: Pair

Learn the two line pattern but 'high ten' your partner on the word **ten** (beat two).

12. 4: Quartet

Two sets of partners create a box, with partners facing each other.

• Pair **A** start
• At the beginning of pair **A**'s line 2, pair **B** start with their line 1.
• Once pair **B**s are in, any **clap and pat** or **round again** will involve a **high five** with the person diagonally to you (not your partner).
• You still **high ten** your partner (beat two).

Suggestion: keep saying the words out loud to your partner — this will help you to keep the rhythm going!

Solo or group rhythms and pieces

for a range of ages

Pieces and polyrhythms

Here is a range of composition and performance ideas aimed at specific age groups.
Feel free to adapt them!

13. A & B with movements

This is a fun polyrhythm that is easily achievable in a short space of time:

14. The Muppet Show with a Shuffle feel

I created this for a BBC children's TV show called *The Let's Go Club*:

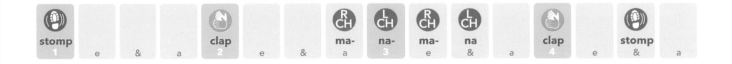

Ideas based on 'Connect It' from BBC *Ten Pieces*

Ten Pieces is a BBC initiative aimed at engaging children in classical music. One of the pieces involved was 'Connect It' by Anna Meredith and David Ogle. Schools were given resources to respond to the work creatively (through music, dance, drama, visual art), and to learn the piece itself. Beat Goes On created a Body Percussion workshop based on 'Connect It' using very physical Body Percussion ostinatos and canons in unusual time signatures (see 'Canon in 7' on page 30).

15. Sumo

R right		CH chest	CH chest	clap		left	and

16. Rainbow

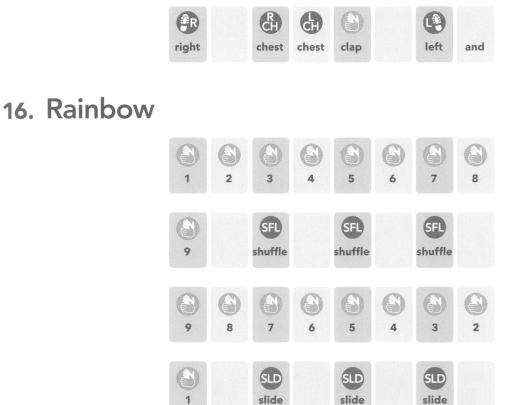

17. Twist

18. All together

Demonstration Video

Afro-Brazilian rhythms

We teach Afro-Brazilian Body Percussion rhythms in our Body Percussion workshops and as a way to learn rhythms when we play on other Percussion instruments. As mentioned in the introduction, Beat Goes On use what we refer to as 'rhythmonics', which is the combination of rhythms and mnemonics. This is a way of verbally learning rhythms, incorporating the rhythms of key words and phrases that relate to the topic. You'll find examples of these in the exercises that follow.

Clave

Clave is a rhythmic motif that features (and influences the structure) in lots of Afro-Cuban and Afro-Brazilian music. There are many variations and as such this is a topic that you can go deeply into if you wish. 3–2 means there are 3 beats in the first half of the bar and 2 in the second half. 2–3 is the opposite.

Here are some of our most frequently used clave patterns:

19. 3–2 Son Clave

20. 2–3 Son Clave

21. 3–2 Bossa nova Clave

22. 2–3 Bossa nova Clave

23. 3–2 Rhumba Clave

24. 2–3 Rhumba Clave

Samba

Samba is an umbrella term for a number of styles including 'pagodé' (a party-style Samba from Rio), 'Bossa nova' (Samba Jazz originating in the 1950s and '60s) and 'Samba Batucada' (the fast, Rio carnival-style Samba). Try these rhythms:

25. Samba swing

26. Partido Alto

27. Marcação

28. All together

Demonstration Video

Samba Reggae

Samba Reggae is a style from Salvador, Bahia, North East Brazil. Notable groups in its development include Ilê Aiyê, Carlinhos Brown's Timbalada and Olodum, the latter of which appeared on Paul Simon's *The Rhythm of the Saints* and Michael Jackson's 'They Don't Care About Us'.

29. Surdo

The Surdo rhythm starts on the fourth beat, on the **Sam-** of 'Samba'. This is also called the 'upbeat'.

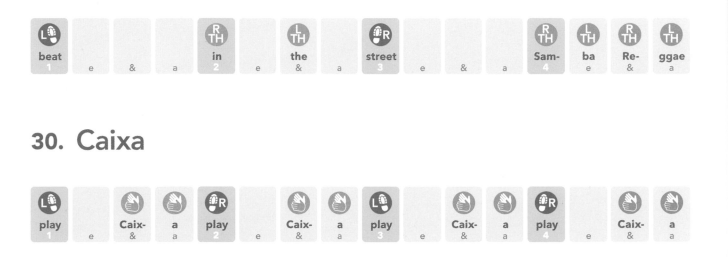

30. Caixa

31. All together

Demonstration Video

Baião

Baião is a rhythm often played on the 'zabumba' drum, and features in Forro, Coco and other styles.

32. Simple

33. Feet and Claps

34. Variation

35. All together

Demonstration Video

Mambo Latin American rhythms and the 'Mambo' from Leonard Bernstein's legendary musical *West Side Story*.

The 'rhythmonics' used describe the nature of the music, a number of Latin American Percussion instruments, numbers in Spanish, and the setting of *West Side Story*.

36. Unison

Unison is a famous section from Bernstein's 'Mambo' and goes over four lines.
The **MAMBO!** is shouted, not clapped.

37. Clave

Clave is a 2–3 Rhumba Clave, and links up with key notes from the 'Cascara' exercise.

38. Cascara

Cascara is a rhythm typically played on the shell of the Timbales when performing the Mambo style.

39. Tumbão

40. All together

Demonstration Video

Maracatu a style from the North East Brazilian state of Pernambuco

This is a folkloric style brought over from West Africa during the time of slavery, then developed in Brazil.

41. Agogo

CH		HIP		CH		HIP		CH	HIP			HIP	CH		HIP	
let	e	the &	a	groove 2	e	flow &	a	on 3	the e	&		A- a	go- 4	e	go &	a

42. Gongue

	play			Gon-		gue			play			Gon-		gue	
1	e	&	a	2	e	&	a	3	e	&	a	4	e	&	a

43. Alfia

L CH	R TH	L TH	R TH	L TH	R TH	L TH	R TH	L TH	R CH	L TH	R TH	L TH	R CH	L TH	R TH
tu 1	Ma- e	ra- &	ca- a	tu 2	Ma- e	ra- &	ca- a	tu 3	Ma- e	ra- &	ca- a	tu 4	Ma- e	ra- &	ca- a

44. All together

Demonstration Video

Other styles and ideas

As well as the Afro-Brazilian rhythms, we can be inspired by other styles such as Hip hop, Funk and Drum'n'bass. Here are a few examples for you to try. With all of them, start slowly and don't be too impatient! You'll get there but it'll take time to get the rhythms flowing smoothly.

45. Solo Groove 1

46. Solo Groove 1 variation

Use your feet to move your body whilst playing the rhythm.
Also, note the click after the right-foot stomp.

47. Solo Groove 2

Emphasise the visual element of this groove by clicking out to each side.

48. Solo Groove 3

Try to get this groove going quickly and smoothly.

49. Solo Groove 4

Try this with a Shuffle feel — you can start with whichever foot you like but keep alternating.

Repeat 3 times

50. Solo Groove 5 based on David Bowie's 'Ashes to Ashes'

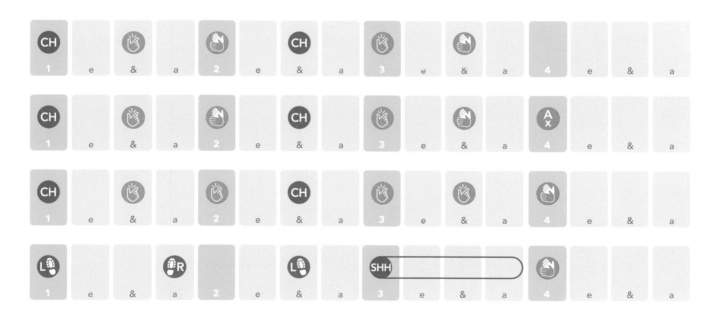

51. Canon in 7

A key feature of Anna Meredith's 'Connect It' from BBC *Ten Pieces* is the use of canons in unusual time signatures — this one is counted in 7.

Each person should learn the line, then stagger their entries against the previous person, coming in on the 'bo-' of 'body'.

With our example here you can create melodies and arpeggios through singing the words.

- Try it with pitches of a scale, indicated in orange below the lyrics. Some people find the whole thing easier with this element included.
- If in a group, try dividing up and have one group singing the whole line on the root note and other groups on the 3rd, 5th and 8th.
- Try the above with and without the Body Percussion.
- Play with dynamics (loud and quiet), texture (how many different things are happening at the same time), and structure (develop these ideas into a piece).

Composing your own pieces

There are several routes to composing your own Body Percussion ideas individually or as a group. In workshops I often use a device called 'Theme & Variation'. I teach an initial rhythmic idea as our 'Theme', and then ask students to add their own flavour to create 'Variations'. I often model some possible variation options and give them opportunities to create their own.

Theme & Variation

Variation options:

Bar/measure 1   – **Theme**
Bar/measure 2   – **Double clap**
Bar/measure 3   – **No clap**
Bar/measure 4   – **Four claps**
Bar/measure 5–8 – **Your own variations on the 'Theme'**

As a group, create one bar/measure of music to be played four times.

- This could played in unison (everyone playing the same thing), or as a polyrhythm (more than one rhythm at the same time).
- Use a slow or medium tempo to start. You can speed up once the rhythm has been composed, if you wish.
- Consider the range of sounds you're going to use, especially when composing two or more rhythms that will be played together.

Think about:

- How will you be arranged as a group?
- Will there be any movement/choreography within your piece? Any time you use your feet you can move: forwards, backwards, to the side, spinning, etc. If you have a two-part polyrhythm, how do they interact with each other?
- Are you saying anything to help you remember you rhythm and sounds e.g. counting beats, saying the body parts, using 'rhythmonics'? Try it — it might help!

Once you're happy playing your music four times through:

- Play it twice through to create an eight-bar/measure section and use a range of dynamics. Experiment with combinations of gradual and sudden changes of dynamic to surprise your audience!
- Build your rhythm up one beat at a time.
- Combine small group work with a unison rhythm that the whole class plays to create a whole-class piece with 'verse' and 'chorus' structure.
- Create a strong ending to finish the piece with a bang!

Use of movement and choreography

The visual element of Percussion is a powerful one — you can see every sound being made. Try to develop this wherever possible. Whenever you stomp, you can also move sideways, forwards, backwards, duck down, twist around. Claps can be above your head, out to the side or underneath legs. How can this be applied in a small or large group settings? Try to make the rhythms look as good as they sound!

Spoken words Body Percussion with literacy

Spoken words can used as great stimuli for rhythmic development. As well as the 'rhythmonics' mentioned earlier, I also use words from literature as a stimulus for Body Percussion composition. This is a fun and kinaesthetic approach that develops confidence and skills with both music and literacy. It has developed out of collaborations with literacy specialist Pie Corbett of Talk4Writing. This approach has also been adapted by teachers of other subject to, for example, help pupils to memorise scientific principles or historical facts. If you work in schools or other education settings, give this a go.

With younger children, start by exploring the rhythms and syllabic elements of their names.

One syllable – '**Sam**', '**Joe**' etc.   Three syllables – '**E-li-sa**', '**Ste-pha-nie**', '**The-o-dore**'
Two syllables – '**Ma-ry**', '**Lu-ca**' etc.   Four syllables   – '**Her-mi-o-ne**', '**E-li-za-beth**'

Which syllable is emphasised — is it '**Ste-PHA-nie**' or '**STE-pha-nie**'?

We then take the phrase '*turning words into Body Percussion*', and give a couple of options of how you can say it out loud over a count of four beats:

Option 1

turn-		ing		words		in-	to	Bo-	dy		Per	cu-	ssion	
1	e	&	a	2	e	&	a	3	e	&	a	4	e	&	a

Option 2

turn-	ing	words					in-		to	Bo-	dy Per	cu-	ssion
1	e	&	a	2	e	&	a	3	e	&	a	4	e	&	a

Get some participants to clap the pulse and the others to say one of the options out loud — this helps to clarify the four beats.

Ask participants to think about which version they prefer and why?
Do you like the regular rhythm of version 1 or the more start-stop, 'syncopated' rhythm of version 2?

Things to note:

- There is no wrong answer, we're simply asking participants to make creative choices.
- In the word 'percussion', is it the middle syllable that is emphasised — 'per-CU-ssion'?
- Version 2 includes 'rests' (musical silences) on the second and third beats. You might want to choose a way to visually (but silently) mark those rests.

In small groups, give each group one line of text each, and the task of deciding how they would like to say their line out loud over a count of four beats.

- Start by saying the words out loud as group as you would do normally.
- With one or two people tapping the pulse, trying fitting the words over four beats as smoothly as possible.
- Do we like the sound of that? If so, why?
- Add a rest on one of the 'pulse' beats — by doing so, you'll have to make the rhythm of the words syncopated for them to fit into the four beats.
- Do you like how it sounds now? Do you prefer the 'regular' rhythm or the 'syncopated' rhythm?

Once the group has decided how their line of text should sound they can try practising it as a group.

Developing the spoken words into Body Percussion

Referring back to our original sentence 'turning words into Body Percussion', split the sentence up into the four beats as follows:

1 – **turning**
2 – **words**
3 – **into**
4 – **Body Percussion**

Choose body sounds for the rhythm of each beat. Once you've decided your four body sounds, practise saying and playing the words and the Body Percussion together.

Having tried this is as a whole class, ask each small group to decide on which body sounds they would like to play on each syllable/word/group of words of their sentence.

• Aim to include three or four different sounds during the course of the sentence
• Combine the words with the rhythm
• Focus on sounds that don't involve hitting the face — these are sensitive areas, and can start to hurt if hitting repeatedly!

Now ask the groups to practise the Body Percussion with the words. This might take a little getting used to but, like with anything, it'll come with practise.

Once the Body Percussion and words are coming along, ask each group to consider:

• How they will arrange themselves as a performing group — in a semicircle, one line, two lines?
• Is there any way they can incorporate movement/choreography into their routine — can they make their routines look as good they sound?

Once each group has developed their Body Percussion routine, ask them to rehearse it together with the words, playing it four times.

• Choose a leader to count the group in at the tempo that they be performing at.
  Use '1, 2, 3, 4', or '1, 2, ready, go'.

Once each group is able to perform their routine, you can start to play around with the words and rhythms. Try the following:

• Words and Body Percussion together
• Words on their own, then Body Percussion, creating a rhythmic echo
• Combining more than one group together — listen to how their routines fit together
• Adjust dynamics — loud, quiet, gradually/suddenly quieter or louder
• Choose one routine for the whole class to play together. You could use this as the 'chorus', and the small group routines as 'verses'.
• Combine all of these elements to create your own whole-class composition and performance.

Feedback and assessment for Body Percussion

Create a list of statements of short term or longer term aims to refer to during the project, e.g.

'Can perform simple Body Percussion rhythms in time, on their own, with a regular sense of pulse'
'Can perform complex syncopated Body Percussion rhythms in a group with a regular sense of pulse'

Use – = + to state pupil progress
+ exceeding the expected standard
= consistently able to meet the expected standard
– working towards the expected standard

You could use 'developing', 'secure' and 'excelling' instead. The use of the word 'expected' obviously allows for differentiation — you might expect a different standard of timekeeping from younger to older students and your statements can vary from project to project.

If you're able to, film all performances, including the delivery of aural and visual feedback — you'll then have clear evidence of progress and assessment for you, your students and your colleagues to refer to.

Suggested stages of progress:

- Hands, simple pattern, in time with group
- Hands, syncopated, in time in group
- Hands, syncopated, maintaining steady tempo independently
- Hands, syncopated using more than one body sound, maintaining steady tempo independently
- Hands, syncopated using more than one sound, as part of polyrhythmic piece
- Hands and feet, simple pattern, in time with group
- Hands and feet, syncopated, in time in group
- Hands and feet, syncopated, maintaining steady tempo independently
- Hands and feet, syncopated, hands using more than one body sound, maintaining steady tempo independently
- Hands and feet, syncopated, hands using more than one sound, as part of polyrhythmic piece.

Links and further resources

There is an ever-growing Body Percussion/Body Music community with new ideas and resources emerging all the time — simply search online. Keith Terry and Crosspulse organise international Body Music festivals, often in collaboration with local groups.
Please visit **www.internationalbodymusicfestival.com** for details.

Música do Círculo 'creates spaces of connection, cooperation and coexistence based on practices of Body Music, non-violent communication, pedagogy of cooperation and collaborative methodologies'.
www.musicadocirculo.com.

'Active Body Beats' is a Body Percussion resource with a strong fitness focus, created by myself and Anna Llombart with Canadian company Kids Into Action in 2015.
For more details, visit **kidsintoaction.ca**.

We also frequently feature videos of our workshops and other Body Percussion content so keep an eye on **www.beatgoeson.co.uk/video** and follow **@BeatGoesOnUK**.

I hope you have found this resource fun, creative and beneficial. If you have any questions or suggestions we'd love to hear from you. If you have any videos of your own ideas we'd love to see and share them so please get in touch via **info@beatgoeson.co.uk**.

Many thanks for your interest, keep the beats going!

Ollie

Thanks

There have been many people and organisations who have given, and continue to give huge support to myself, Beat Goes On, and the creating of this resource.

Sam Alexander
Charlie Beale
Martin Owens
Mike Johnson
Pat White
Carnival Collective crew, past and present!
Mestre Mags and LSS
The Scottish samba massive!
Keith Terry and the body music community worldwide
Luke Cresswell, Steve McNicholas and all the awesome STOMP and Lost & Found Orchestra
performers, crew and workshop facilitators I've had the pleasure of performing and teaching with.
Marianna Hay and Orchestras For All members past and present
Mike and all at Inspire Works
Pie Corbett and Talk4Writing
All Little Kids Rockers
Musical Futures UK & International
BSME, COBIS and LAHC
Shelly Ambury and all at Sing Up
Catherine Barker
All at Charanga
All at Ikon Arts
Music Mark
Musicians Union
BBC Ten Pieces
Nathan Theodoulou
Anna Gower
Anna Rusbatch
Emily Sayers
Dan Griffiths
Katherine Sowerby
Jane Humberstone
Andy Casterton
Helen Battelley
Graeme Hare
John, Lucy and all at ESM Inbound
Graham Padmore
Tom Lydon and all at Hal Leonard
Patrick Lawrence
Team BGO — Gina Abolins, Lily May, Alua Nascimento, Lee Crisp, Mika De Oliveira, Raz Jayasuriya,
Fred Claridge, Fernando Machado, Alba Cabral, Tiziana Pozzo, Lil Iontcheva, Sam Alexander
(again!), Adrian Wiggins, Anna Llombart, Blake Vickers, Silas Mosbacher, Art Brasil and Global Grooves.

All the amazing music education hub staff, arts organisations, teachers and students I have had,
and continue to have, the pleasure of working with throughout the UK and internationally!

Daisy and my whole family, who have continuously supported my musical goings on.
Without you this resource simply wouldn't exist — thank you. xxx